THE NORTH AMERICAN RIVER OTTER
PLAYFUL SLIDER

by Barbara Juster Esbensen
Illustrated by Mary Barrett Brown

LITTLE, BROWN AND COMPANY
Boston · Toronto · London

Also by Barbara Juster Esbensen and Mary Barrett Brown
GREAT NORTHERN DIVER
The Loon

A little otter in Eureka, California,
captured my affection long ago.
This book is for her.
B.J.E.

To Kathy and Chris—
whose joyous nature reminds me of
the playful slider.
M.B.B.

My thanks to Chris Kline, zoologist, Minnesota Trail, at the Minnesota Zoo, for his kindness and his interest in this book. He took me behind the scenes to meet the otters, to listen to their various calls, and to note details about their behavior and interaction with one another.

The zoo's marvelous otter exhibit gave me a privileged view of the underwater life of these delightful animals — an experience no amount of seeking them in the wild would provide.
B.J.E.

A special thank-you to Jason Kallsen, whose photographs of otters were invaluable to me.

And, as always, my love and gratitude to Porter and Bevy, who never fail to come to my rescue.
M.B.B.

First Edition

Library of Congress Cataloging-in-Publication Data

Esbensen, Barbara Juster.
  Playful slider : the North American river otter / by Barbara Juster Esbensen ;
illustrated by Mary Barrett Brown. — 1st ed.
    p.   cm.
  Summary: Explores the world of the North American river otter, describing the playful mammal's behavior and characteristics.
  ISBN 0-316-24977-7
  1. Lutra canadensis — Juvenile literature. [1. Otters.] I. Brown, Mary Barrett, ill. II. Title.
QL737.C25E82 1993
599. 74'447 — dc20   92-13783

10 9 8 7 6 5 4 3 2 1

WOR

Published simultaneously in Canada
by Little, Brown & Company (Canada) Limited

Printed in the United States of America

At the bottom of the river
is an otter
wearing golden shoes.

— *from an ancient Latvian folk song*

It is a glittering winter day, so cold that other animals are curled deep in their dens. But the fresh tracks of two otters are printed on the new-fallen snow. The pair has left the frozen river where they have been swimming after fish under the ice.

Now they are hunting small mammals and come to the top of a hill. Any hill is irresistible to an otter, and this snowy slope drops down to the river below.

The two otters abandon the hunt and push off, holding their legs close to their bodies as they whizz along. Snow crystals fly up into their bright eyes. Sometimes they stick one foot out in front to steer around a bush or a rock. Suddenly the hill takes a steeper plunge. The otters push both forefeet straight out in front to slow their rushing slide onto the river ice. Then up the slippery hill they struggle — ready to do it all over again!

Otters are probably best known for what seems to be their sense of fun. Most mammals romp and play when they are very young. But even adult otters spend a large portion of every day looking for things to play with and places to slide.

badger

fisher

marten

skunk

wolverine

mink

Otters belong to the Mustelidae, or weasel, family, but they do not behave like their relatives. Mustelids include skunks, fishers, badgers, martens, wolverines, and mink. All of these animals are fierce, aggressive, and often short-tempered.

But otters, who can live to be twenty years old, behave quite differently. Play is important to these lively animals. They can keep it up for hours!

At last the two otters are tired of belly-sliding down the hill. As if on a signal, they both plunge headfirst under the snow. Silence. No sound cuts the frosty air. Nothing moves.

Suddenly: "*Chirp!*" A black nose pops up out of the white field, followed by whiskers, head, and long body. The otter sits up on its back legs and tail to look around. It chirps again. Not far away, another head pokes through the snow. "*Whuh! Whuh!*" it answers. And as soon as it hears this sound, the first otter dives under the snow and disappears.

Only the deep churning snow gives away the furious, buried hide-and-seek chase. When at last the two otters come together, they send the snow flying in a frantic wrestling match.

Finally the pair romps off together, ready to return to their den in the riverbank.

Although river otters love to be in, under, and around bodies of water, their short legs can carry them very well on land. They have an awkward walk and almost always run, humping up their backs and then straightening out again — almost like an inchworm. North American river otters have four rough bumps on the pads of their hind feet. These bumps give good traction on slippery surfaces. While the otter is slow compared with a deer or bobcat, it can outrun a human.

The river otter is easy to recognize. It is long and slender like other members of the weasel family. Most of its fur is a rich, glossy brown, but its lips, chin, cheeks, and throat are lighter. It has a wide, flat head and a short muzzle.

Its nose is large, black, and bulblike. It has brown eyes and small, rounded ears. When it swims underwater, the otter can close its nostrils, and it can also shut its ears with tiny flaps.

The otter's stiff, sensitive whiskers are connected with large nerve pads. These whiskers probably help otters locate and catch their prey and allow them to test the width of an opening before they try to enter it. Thirty-six teeth tear, cut, and grind the flesh, shells, and bones of its prey.

The muscular neck seems to flow into the rest of the otter's lean body. The long, wide tail tapers to a point.

The otter's main food is fish, and its streamlined brown body makes it a powerful underwater swimmer. Its tail acts like a rudder as the animal's muscular body and webbed feet propel it underwater as fast and as gracefully as a seal. The otter is the fastest swimmer of any freshwater mammal. Only the loon can match it for underwater speed.

Otters usually live in one or more abandoned dens they take over from

another animal. These dens are almost always near water. The otter makes one entrance under the water. A tunnel leads up to a chamber that sits well above the water level. This is where the female otter makes the nest. Often there is another chamber off to the side to be used as a toilet area. There is an entrance above ground as well. This gives the otters two ways to enter the den and provides ventilation to the underground chambers.

As the ponds and rivers freeze, otters use only their underwater entrance to come and go from the den. All during the hard freeze of winter, they are active, swimming under the ice searching for food. They must breathe air every few minutes. They use pockets of air that form under the ice, and they can return to the den to breathe the air that comes in through the opening above ground.

Even in the coldest weather, the den stays warm because it is under the earth and out of the wind and storms.

Sometimes otters will find water that does not freeze at all, and more than one family of otters will fish and play in the same open water. They all seem to get along. Otters act as though the more bodies they can chase, snuggle, wrestle, and curl up with, the better.

Even though most of the otter's food comes from the water, it will eat many things besides fish: crayfish, insects (including wasps), turtles, snakes, snails, freshwater clams, freshwater shrimp, small mammals, and an occasional duck.

As soon as the river otter catches food in the water, it returns to dry land to eat it. When it comes ashore, its fur looks spiky and rough. The otter then rolls on the ground or in the snow to dry off.

Although otters spend a great deal of time in the water, their fur is not waterproof. Air trapped among the hairs keep it insulated, but if the otter were to stay in the water too long, its fur would gradually become waterlogged.

Like all mustelids, the otter has a scent gland, which can give off a strong odor. Otters leave their scent on tufts of grass or on mounds of mud and leaves. These are called scenting stations. The scent tells other otters when a female is ready for breeding. It can tell a male otter when there is a rival male nearby. The scenting station provides all kinds of information to otters who are passing by.

Otters mate in the spring, but the fertilized eggs do not begin to develop until much later in the year. Although scientists cannot be sure, the eggs probably start to develop in December or January. This delay means that the young are not born until the following spring, when the weather is warm enough to be safe for newborn cubs.

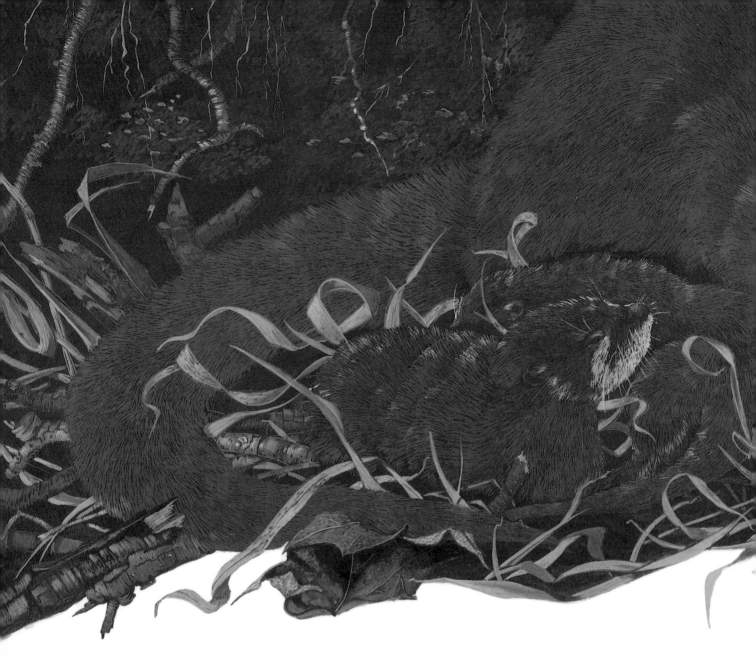

When the time is near for her to give birth, the female will line the dry chamber of one of the more hidden dens with grasses and leaves. She may make it bigger so that it is the right size for her new family.

There are usually two or three cubs, but sometimes an otter will have a litter of as many as five.

The cubs are blind and toothless and do not open their eyes until they are about five weeks old. The young weigh about four ounces at birth and have fur and claws and whiskers. They are miniature otters, with a two-and-a-half-inch tail that looks just like the tail of an adult. Including this tail, the babies are about nine inches long. When they are full-grown, they will be from thirty to forty-eight inches long including the tail — which may be as long as twenty inches! The male cubs will be quite a bit larger than the females. They can weigh over thirty pounds when they are adults.

When the young are born, the mother chases the father out of the den and takes great care with her cubs, feeding them and licking them clean. She curls her body around the babies to keep them warm. Like all mammals, she provides them with her milk. This milk is very rich, and the young otters grow rapidly.

For many weeks after her cubs are born, the mother otter keeps them isolated in the den. Although they are getting bigger every day, the little otters, like the young of all predators, develop very slowly. When they are about thirty-five days old, their eyes open, but they are quite helpless until they are around six weeks old.

At this age, they begin to tumble and play with each other and with their mother. An otter's five toes are as nimble as fingers, and cubs spend some of their playtime rolling pebbles around and around from paw to paw. A cub might juggle a chunk of food or a piece of wood — or balance food on the end of its nose!

But they must wait until they are three or four months old before their mother will allow them to play outside the den.

Even after she takes them outside, the mother is careful to protect them from any possible danger. The father is not allowed to come near until the cubs are about six months of age.

Once the young otters have grown their thick adult coats, the mother must teach them to swim. Although they like to play in shallow water, splashing and chasing one another, the young cubs must be coaxed away from land into water deep enough for them to swim in.

This is not easy. The cubs resist. They squeal and try to stay on the shore. The mother often has to drag a shrieking cub by the scruff of the neck out into the deep water. She sometimes swims with the cub riding on her back. When she is out far enough, she sinks, and the cub must paddle and thrash and keep itself afloat. The mother stays close by to rescue it if it gets into trouble.

The young otters learn to swim quickly once they have lost their fear
of deep water. Soon they are part of a swimming, diving, chasing, romping
crowd of boisterous relatives. Otters make whole playgrounds of muddy slides
leading from steep banks into the water.

They chase one another and hide underwater, ducking out of sight and
popping up again with a chirp or a whuffing snort. "*Whuh! Whuh! Whuh!*"
they call to one another and then dive out of sight before poking their heads
up somewhere else.

Adult river otters have few if any natural enemies. Nothing can catch them in the water, and on land they are very hard to handle. Without fear or a minute of hesitation, a twenty-pound otter will take on a ninety-pound dog. The otter's muscular body, its endurance, and its powerful jaws and teeth will send the opponent running for cover.

Otters stay in one general area in the summer, when food is in great abundance. With the warm days bringing out insects of all kinds and with streams and lakes filled with food, the parents begin to teach the cubs how to catch

The cubs soon learn how to outswim a fish and corner it in a hole along the bank. But much of an otter's food must be rooted out of the mud and debris at the bottom of the pond or lake. Frogs live there, as well as turtles, crayfish, mud minnows, and aquatic insects.

Otters are so buoyant that they have to make a strong effort to stay down near the bottom to feed. When it is rooting around in the mud, the otter is nearly vertical — nose down, tail up. It must keep its hind feet moving constantly so that it doesn't float to the surface!

When the adult otter goes after a fish, its sleek, dark body speeds like a swift shadow beneath the surface of the stream. Silvery bubbles cling to its fur and trail out behind it. When it bursts out of the water, the glistening prey is clamped in its jaws.

Autumn. The days grow colder, and the otter family begins to move around, covering more territory. The cubs are almost full-grown and travel about with their mother and father, inspecting the countryside. They will stay with their parents through the winter but will leave in the spring before the new litter of cubs is born.

The first heavy snowfall again covers the riverbank and the fields above their den. The otter family bounds across the meadow, leaving patterns of run-and-slide, run-and-slide in the new snow. They scramble up to the top of the hill, one after the other, and shove off. Another morning of downhill belly-flopping has begun for this family of playful sliders.